Double Danger: Thunderstorms and Tornadoes

by Laura T. Johnson

 HOUGHTON MIFFLIN HARCOURT

PHOTOGRAPHY CREDITS: COVER ©Scott Tysick/Getty Images; ©Photodisc/Getty Images; 3 (b) ©Classic Image/Alamy Images; 6 (bg) Comstock/Getty Images; 7 (b) ©PictureArts/Corbis; 9 (r) ©Scott Tysick/Getty Images; 10 (bg) ©Comstock Images/Getty Images; 14 ©Flickr RF/Getty Images

Printed in China

ISBN: 978-0-544-07297-8

12 13 14 15 0940 20 19 18 17

4500693652   A B C D E F G

Contents

Vocabulary	Stretch Vocabulary
precipitation	tornado
water cycle	

Introduction

When it's raining hard, people often say, "It's raining cat and dogs." Cats and dogs have never fallen from the sky during a storm, but other animals have. In 1882, it "rained" frogs in Iowa. In 2010, it "rained" fish in Australia.

All around the world, there have been reports of frogs, fish, and other small animals falling from the sky during storms. They were not true precipitation that fell from clouds. But they did fall with rain or hail.

How this can happen? To find out, you need to know about thunderstorms and tornadoes.

In 1858, fish fell from the sky in Nikolaisberg, Transylvania.

Inside a Thundercloud

The water cycle is the continual movement of water back and forth between Earth's surface and the atmosphere. Water changes form as this movement occurs. The water evaporates and becomes water vapor. The water vapor rises and condenses or freezes to form clouds.

When a storm happens, strong winds at the bottom of clouds can blow water droplets high into the cloud, where the droplets freeze. Wind at the top of the cloud blows the ice back down to the bottom of the cloud.

Water and other kinds of matter contain particles with electrical charges. As the ice and water move past each other, the ice takes some of the electrical charge from the water.

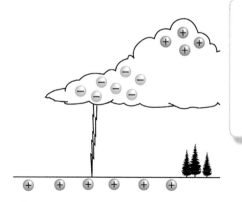

In lightning, a cloud forms areas of positive (+) charge and negative (-) charge. The ground below the cloud becomes positively charged.

A flash of lightning releases a large amount of energy.

The ice carries the charge down to the bottom of the cloud. In time, the bottom of the cloud builds up a very strong electrical charge. When the charge becomes strong enough, it can jump through the air to the ground or to another cloud. That is lightning.

Lightning releases lots of energy. One kind of energy that lightning releases is light. That's why a flash of lightning can light up a large area. Lightning also releases intense heat. That's why lightning can start fires.

Lightning Facts

Where does lightning strike? Lightning can travel within a cloud, between clouds, or between a cloud and Earth's surface. Cloud-to-surface lightning might strike the ground, a tree, a mountain, or a building.

How often does lightning strike? Lightning is more common than you might think. As you read this, lightning will strike about 2,000 times around the world.

How dangerous is lightning? Lightning is extremely dangerous. In the United States, about 100 people are killed every year by lightning or fires caused by lightning.

This is cloud-to-cloud lightning. It stretches across the sky, not down to the ground.

Thunder

Lightning causes thunder. When lightning travels through the air, the intense heat from the lightning causes the air around it to expand quickly. This sudden tunnel of expanded air is called a channel.

Once the lightning passes through this channel, the air cools. The cooling of the air causes the tunnel to collapse quickly. The expansion and collapse release loud sound energy that we hear as thunder.

Light travels much faster than sound, so we see the lightning flash before we hear the thunder. Count the seconds between the flash and the thunder and divide them by five. That's how many miles away the lightning is!

Thunder is the sound created when the air expands and then collapses very quickly.

Thunderstorm Safety

Thunderstorms can be very dangerous. As you know, they produce lightning. Thunderstorms also create strong winds that create dangers, such as falling trees.

If a thunderstorm is approaching, try to go inside a building, and follow the safety tips below.

Lightning Safety Tips

- Keep away from windows and doors.

- Turn off the television and the computer. Don't use electrical appliances.

- Stay away from sinks and tubs and anything else connected to water.

If you must stay outside, squat low in an open area. Place your hands over your head and ears. If you are in a group of people, spread out. Stay about 15 feet away from one another.

Don't swim. Stay away from any kind of water, such as a pool, a lake, or the ocean.

If you can't find shelter, be sure to stay away from trees. Lightning often strikes the tallest object in an area. The electricity can travel down a tree and into the ground where you are standing.

Lightning often strikes tall trees. Stay twice as far from a tree as it is tall.

Tornadoes

Tornadoes—also called *twisters*—are among nature's most powerful and destructive storms. Tornadoes can rip roofs off of houses and shatter large buildings. They can pull huge trees out of the ground and break them into pieces. They can toss large objects, such as cars and trucks, into the air. Tornadoes can kill people.

Tornadoes often skip across the ground, destroying some things and leaving others untouched. A tornado can last a few seconds or more than an hour.

Tornadoes look like funnel-shaped clouds hanging down from thunderclouds.

How Tornadoes Form

Tornadoes usually form inside thunderclouds. Warm, moist air rises from the ground and passes through colder air in these clouds. The rising warm air at the bottom of the cloud is pushed by winds from different directions and begins to spin. The spinning motion creates a column of air.

As the column of air spins faster and faster, it gets longer. A funnel or cone of spinning air drops from the bottom of the cloud and reaches toward the ground. When it touches the ground, it becomes a tornado.

A tornado occurs when a rapidly spinning column of air extends from a cloud to the ground.

The Speed of a Tornado

The Beaufort Scale can be used to estimate wind speed based on the effects of the wind. The scale reaches up to hurricane-force winds, which are 120 kilometers per hour (75 mph) or more. Since the wind inside a tornado can be four times faster, we use a different scale—the Fujita Scale. Tornadoes themselves travel at about 55 kilometers per hour (35 mph) over the ground.

The United States has more tornadoes every year than any other country. They occur most frequently in an area called "Tornado Alley."

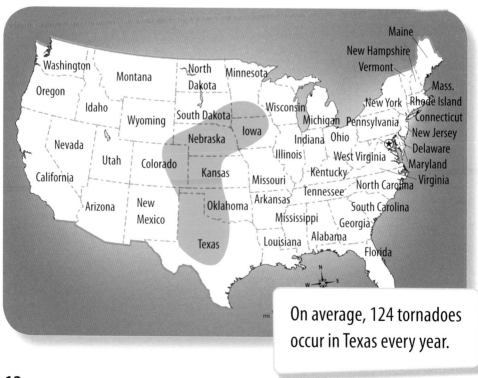

On average, 124 tornadoes occur in Texas every year.

Here are some safety tips to follow if there is a tornado headed toward your area.

Tornado Safety Tips

▶ Go to the basement of your house. Crawl under something strong, such as a table or workbench. Cover yourself with something soft that will protect you from falling objects. A mattress is a good choice.

▶ If you don't have a basement, go to a small room such as a bathroom or closet. Stay away from windows.

▶ If you are at school, your teacher will lead you to an inner hallway. Kneel on the floor. Keep your head down and protect the back of your head with your hands.

This position is important because it can help protect you from falling objects.

Waterspouts

Waterspouts are tornadoes that move over water. As they pass over water, they can siphon up water and other things. Waterspouts can carry objects a long distance before letting them fall to the ground, along with rain or hail.

Have you guessed that this is how the frogs and fish fell to the ground during the storms you read about on page 3? Yes, waterspouts picked them up, carried them to a new location, and let them fall like rain.

Waterspouts are tornadoes that siphon up water and carry it with them.

Observe and Record Wind Force

Ask your teacher for a copy of the Beaufort Scale.
Go outside on five different days and observe
the wind. Does it move leaves on trees? Does
it bend small branches? Can it sway trees? Find
the description on the Beaufort Scale that best
fits what you observe. Make a chart that shows
the date and the Beaufort Scale number for
each day. Add a sentence or two describing your
observations.

Create a School Storm-Safety Poster

Make a poster for your school that shows how to
stay safe in a thunderstorm or a tornado. Write
safety instructions and draw pictures to illustrate
them. If your school has a storm shelter or a
special place to go during a storm, explain how
to get there.

Glossary

precipitation [pri•SIP•uh•TAY•shuhn] Water that falls from clouds to Earth's surface. Rain, snow, sleet, and hail are forms of precipitation.

tornado [tohr•NAY•doh] A powerful, twisting column of air dropping down from a cloud to the ground.

water cycle [WAW•ter SY•kuhl] The movement of water from Earth's surface to the air and back again.